School Rules Are....?

By Ymkje Wideman-van der Laan
Illustrated by Jennifer Lackgren

For Logan

When I came home from school one day,
I didn't get much time to play.
I did not finish my work, you see,
So teacher sent it home with me.

On teacher's daily report she said,
My behavior had also been quite bad.
I didn't listen, got angry, and screeched.
Quite a few school rules I had breached.

My grandma said it's not so smart
When school rules I don't take to heart.
Schools have rules for a very good reason:
They help kids learn and progress each season.

I knew there were rules for home and when out.
I have rules for playtime and running about.
I know what to do when I ride in a car,
But I had to ask, "Grandma, school rules are…?"

We sat down together with paper and pen,
And Grandma wrote down these school rules then.
I am going to learn them, and practice them, too,
'Cause Grandma says that's the right thing to do.

Good Eyes

Good Ears

Good Hands

Good Feet

Good Voice

Good Friends

Good Eyes

Look at your teacher, and pay attention.
That way your teacher won't have to mention
To concentrate, and do your best,
So you'll finish your work, and pass each test.

Listen closely when your teacher asks
That you follow directions and stick to your tasks.
If you do things right, you may get a reward.
You could even earn a Good Student Award.

Good Hands

Use your hands to color or write.
Don't toss or throw, hold your pencil tight.
Don't crumple your paper, but do your work well.
Keep hands to yourself 'til you hear the bell.

Good Feet

Stay in your seat, don't get up and roam,
Unless it is recess, or time to go home.
When walking in hallways, go with the flow.
Don't run or sit down, walk nice and slow.

Good Voice

Please talk softly,
don't yell or shout.
That disturbs your friends,
and is much too loud.

Be sure to be nice,
and give compliments.

Say "please" and
"thank you" to teachers
and friends.

Good Friends

Be good to your friends,
and always be kind.
Be helpful and caring,
and you will find,

That every good and
nice thing that you do,
Your friends will return
and do back to you.

Ryleigh, Logan's cousin and best friend, drew 10 little pencils and hid them in the pages of this book. Can you find them?

About the Author

Ymkje Wideman-van der Laan is a writer, editor, and proofreader. In 2006, she assumed the care of her 6-month old grandson, Logan. There were signs of autism at an early age, and the diagnosis became official in 2009. She has been his advocate, and passionate about promoting autism awareness ever since. Logan is the inspiration behind *School Rules Are...?* and other children's books she wrote for him. You can find out more about her and her books at www.ymkje.com and www.autism-is.com.

Note to Parents and Caregivers

Keeping to and focusing on a task, staying seated, and transitioning from one activity or place to another while in school, can be challenging for children with autism. It certainly was for my grandson when he started attending school.

We were very fortunate to have the help and expertise of Ron Gibson, MA CAS, the lead school psychologist and chairperson of the Autism Problem Solving Team for Harnett County Schools, N.C. He and his team developed some basic school rules for children with autism, and the teachers introduced these rules to my grandson's class. To help reinforce the rules he was learning at school, I wrote *School Rules Are...?* I also made some simple illustrated visual supports to go along with each rule. My grandson, and the other children in his class, soon caught on, and *Good Eyes, Good Ears, Good Hands, Good Feet, Good Voice, Good Friends,* became household words.

Verbally and visually reminding my grandson of the rules regularly and consistently, both at home and in the classroom, continues to make a big difference and helps his time at school to be successful and productive. I hope *School Rules Are...?* with its bold and bright illustrations can help do the same for other children with autism.

The Author

School Rules Are...? Visual Supports

Following are some easy-to-make visual supports that you can use along with the *School Rules Are...?* book, should you so desire.*

To prepare the *School Rules Are...?* Key Ring Cards, cut out the cards along the dotted lines before laminating them. Leave at least ½ inch between each card as you put them in the laminating pouches, so when you cut them after laminating, there is about ¼ inch of lamination on all sides. Punch a hole in the corner of each card where indicated, and put them in order on a 1-inch loose leaf ring, or book ring.

Use the Key Ring Cards at home to teach the school rules, and review them daily, or however often you feel would be helpful for your child. Also show the *School Rules Are...?* Key Ring Cards to your child's teacher, and ask him/her to use the same set of rules at school.

To make it easy for the teacher to commend your child, or remind your child of a rule during class time, cut out and laminate a couple of task strips for him/her. The teacher can tape one to your child's desk, and carry a spare one with him/her for the times your child is not in the classroom. The teacher can simply point to a picture on the task strip to praise your child for good behavior, or if necessary, remind your child of a rule along with a brief verbal instruction. For example, if your child is listening well in class, the teacher can point to the corresponding picture and say, "Good Ears! You're listening very well!" Or before transitioning out of the classroom, he/she can point to the corresponding picture and say, "Remember, Good Feet!"

I hope that making these visual supports available to you will make your life just a little easier, and will contribute to your child's success at school.

The Author

*In case you prefer to leave these pages in the book, these visual supports, and an additional *School Rules Are...?* mini-poster, are also available for downloading and printing from www.autism-is.com.

School Rules Are...?

Good Eyes

Good Ears

Good Hands

Look at your teacher,
and pay attention.
That way your teacher
won't have to mention
To concentrate, and do
your best,
So you'll finish your
work, and pass each test.

Use your hands to
color or write.
Don't toss or throw,
hold your pencil tight.
Don't crumple your
paper, but do your
work well.
Keep hands to yourself
'til you hear the bell.

Listen closely when your
teacher asks
That you follow directions
and stick to your tasks.
If you do things right,
you may get a reward.
You could even earn a
Good Student Award.

Good Feet

Good Voice

Good Friends

Good Eyes

Good Ears

Good Hands

Good Feet

Good Voice

Good Friends

Please talk softly,
don't yell or shout.
That disturbs your friends,
and is much too loud.
Be sure to be nice,
and give compliments.
Say please and thank you
to teachers and friends.

Stay in your seat,
don't get up and roam,
Unless it is recess,
or time to go home.
When walking in
hallways,
go with the flow.
Don't run or sit down,
walk nice and slow.

Be good to your friends,
and always be kind.
Be helpful and caring,
and you will find,
That every good and
nice thing that you do,
Your friends will return
and do back to you.

For more information and other products,
visit www.autism-is.com.

Task Strips

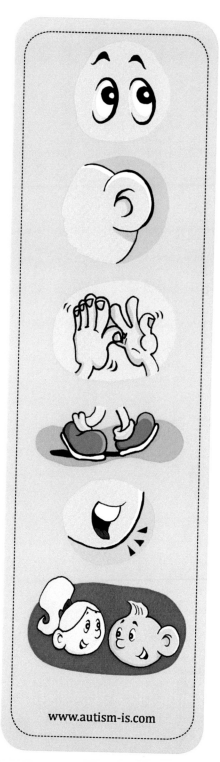

www.autism-is.com

www.autism-is.com

www.autism-is.com

Made in the USA
San Bernardino, CA
20 June 2019